ARTHUR EVANS AND THE P.

Cover photograph: Arthur Evans watching the restoration of
the Grand Staircase

Frontispiece: Drawing of Sir Arthur Evans in 1937, by Robin Guthrie

UNIVERSITY OF OXFORD
ASHMOLEAN MUSEUM

ARTHUR EVANS

AND THE

PALACE OF MINOS

ANN BROWN

ASHMOLEAN MUSEUM OXFORD
1994

ASHMOLEAN MUSEUM PUBLICATIONS

Archaeology, History and Classical studies

Treasures of the Ashmolean
Archaeology, Artefacts and the Bible
Ancient Cyprus
Ancient Egypt
Ancient Italy
The Ancient Romans
The Ancient Near East
Ancient Greek Terracottas
The Arundel Marbles
Greek Vases
Scythian Treasures in Oxford
Sir Arthur Evans: a Memoir
The Content Cameos

Text and illustrations
© Ashmolean Museum, Oxford 1983

ISBN 0 9000 9092 8   Paperback
ISBN 0 907849 50 4   Hardback

Designed by Andrew Ivett and typeset in
Palatino by Midas Publishing Services Ltd,
Oxford

Printed and bound in Great Britain at
The Bath Press (formerly The Pitman Press),
Bath, 1983. Reprinted 1986, 1989, and 1994.

Contents

Notes and Acknowledgements

All the objects illustrated are in the Department of Antiquities unless otherwise stated. The numbers which appear in brackets in the plate captions are the serial numbers in the accessions registers in the Department of Antiquities; the prefix AE stands for Aegean.

The photographs are kept in the Department of Antiquities and are published here by courtesy of the Keeper.

The Evans and Mackenzie Notebooks are in the Ashmolean Library and excerpts are reproduced by courtesy of the Ashmolean Library Committee

I am deeply indebted to Sinclair Hood for his help during the preparation of the text and plates and to John Boardman for his help and encouragement. I should also like to thank the Keeper of the Department of Antiquities, Humphrey Case, and my colleagues, David Brown, Elizabeth MacRobert, Mervyn Popham and Michael Vickers for their helpful comments. Pat Clarke designed the cover and Denise Griffin has been responsible for the photographic work, Hilary Frame helped me sort out much of the archival material; I am grateful for all their skill and patience. I should also like to thank Gerald Cadogan for allowing me to use the plan of the Palace (p. 8) from *Palaces of Minoan Crete*, 56–7. Finally I should like to thank Peggy Gilson and Françoise Holt for their careful typing.

I am grateful to the following for permission to reprint previously published material — The Delegates of the Oxford University Press (*Hazel* and *The Antiquaries Journal* vol vii (1927)), Dr. T.M. Schuller, Executor of Dame Joan Evans (*Time and Chance*), and the Trustees of the Estate of Sir Arthur Evans (*The Palace of Minos*).

Foreword

The Ashmolean Museum is well known to possess the most representative collection of Minoan antiquities outside Crete, a major part of which came to the Department of Antiquities from excavations made over a number of years from 1900 onwards by Sir Arthur Evans, who was Keeper of the Museum from 1884 until 1908 and closely associated with the Museum until his death in 1941. It is less well known that the Ashmolean Library (in the same building as the Museum) possesses the excavators' notebooks and that the Department of Antiquities holds their photographic records. Between them, these archives describe and illustrate the progress not only of the excavations but also of the concurrent reconstructions of the Palace made under Evans's direction. Ann Brown makes a selection from these archives widely available for the first time; with their aid and with the help of contemporary newspaper and other accounts, she provides a fascinating picture of the conduct of exceptionally important excavations and insight into reconstructions, which yearly impress thousands of visitors to Crete and continue to excite scholarly interest and controversy.

Humphrey Case,
Keeper of Antiquities,
Ashmolean Museum.

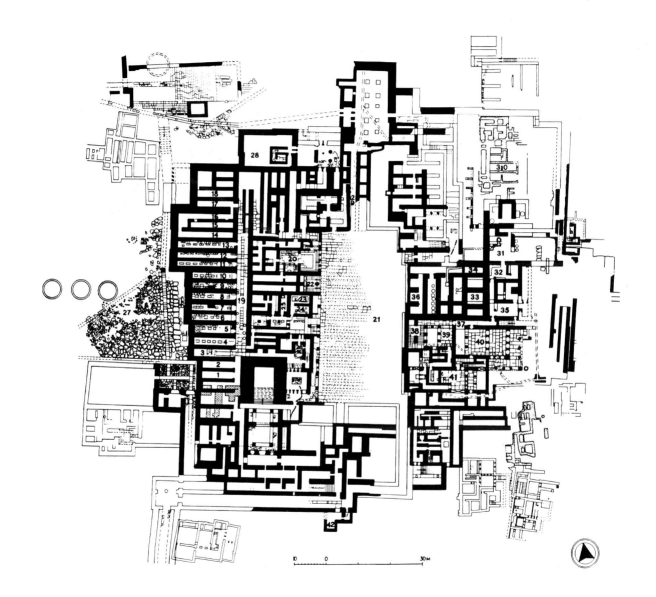

9

Chronology

The chronology used here is that proposed by Evans who coined the term Minoan after King Minos, the legendary ruler of Crete. The term refers to both a period and a style of pottery and is divided into Early, Middle and Late Minoan; these in turn are sub-divided. The alternative terminology is based on the cultural and architectural developments classified as Palatial.

		Approximate dates BC
EARLY MINOAN I EARLY MINOAN II EARLY MINOAN III MIDDLE MINOAN IA	PRE-PALATIAL	3000–2000
	———	
MIDDLE MINOAN IB MIDDLE MINOAN II	First Palaces built PROTO-PALATIAL, PERIOD OF THE OLD OR EARLY PALACES Palaces destroyed	2000–1700
	———	
MIDDLE MINOAN III LATE MINOAN I	rebuilding of the Palaces NEO-PALATIAL, PERIOD OF THE NEW OR LATER PALACES	1700–1400
LATE MINOAN II	———	
LATE MINOAN III	POST-PALATIAL MYCENAEAN	1400–1100

Introduction

The photographs used to illustrate this picture book have been taken from the Photographic Archives of the Department of Antiquities, Ashmolean Museum, Oxford. Most are prints made from negatives from the collection of Sir Arthur Evans, many of the photographs having been taken by Marayiannis, a photographer from Candia (Heraklion), Crete (at considerable expense (pl. 4)), and by Theodore Fyfe, one of the site architects. Others come from Noel Heaton's collection, which was recently transferred to the Ashmolean from the Institute of Archaeology, University of London. Heaton visited Crete 'bringing his expert chemical and technical knowledge to bear on a minute and careful analysis of the painted stucco'. Many of the prints in the Ashmolean remain unpublished, but some have been used to illustrate in particular the excavation reports in the *Annual of the British School at Athens* vols. vi–xi (1900–1906), and the *Palace of Minos* (1921–1935). Various scholars have used the prints to illustrate more recent research.

Evans used photographs not only in his publications but also in the exhibitions for which he was responsible. Cretan material, largely prints, plans and casts, was first displayed at Burlington House, London in 1903, when readers of the *Guardian* (14.1.'03) were told 'This part of the exhibition closes at the end of January, so all those who wish to see with their own eyes that the "myth" of Minos and Daedalus, and the Labyrinth had a very solid foundation, had better visit the Academy betimes'. Popular demand ensured that the exhibition stayed on view until mid-March. A major exhibition also held in Burlington House commemorated the Jubilee of the British School at Athens in 1936 (pls. 1,2), and many photographs were incorporated there and in the permanent exhibition in the Ashmolean Museum which Evans mounted with the help of Mercy Money-Coutts, completing the display in 1939 at the age of 88. Negatives were made into slides for the many lectures he gave. In the audience of one given in conjunction with the British School at Athens Jubilee Exhibition was a schoolboy, Michael Ventris, whose involvement with the decipherment of the Linear B script was to have momentous results (p. 54). Evans has been described as an unimpressive lecturer but his lectures to the less academic must have been lively and entertaining to judge from his skeleton notes, some of which are now in the Ashmolean. They included pictures of the site and of objects. The last four slides in a talk delivered at Bath College on January 30th, 1905 were 'Workmen' (pl. 6b), 'Tug of War' (pl. 9), 'Choros' (pl. 10a), and 'Our Boys'. Similar slides provided light relief at his lecture (p. 35) in the Parish Room at Wootton, Boars Hill, Oxford, and included the donkey on the site, which had to be driven off before excavation could begin.

Thousands of visitors enjoy going round the restored Palace at Knossos each year and many must inevitably wonder whether the restoration is the work of Evans' imagination or based on more solid evidence. This picture book makes no attempt to judge the issue, but by using contemporary photographs it shows various areas of the Palace in the course of restoration, or 'reconstruction' as Evans preferred to term it. The choice of areas is somewhat arbitrary. Some of the prints chosen show the provenance of objects now in the Ashmolean, others are of areas particularly well documented by the photographs in the Museum archives. The Grand Staircase is one such area and this has been dealt with in more detail (77ff.).

The photographs chosen are confined to the Palace site at Knossos. The Palace was built early in the Middle Minoan Period and was both an administrative centre and a ruler's residence. The aim of Evans' reconstruction was both to protect the fabric of the buildings from the extremes of the Cretan weather and to present to the visitor a view of the Later Palace as it might have appeared in its original state. This second or later Palace was re-built, after a devastating destruction, about 1700 BC. A great Stepped Portico provided access to the Palace from the south for travellers coming from the interior of the island. An entrance to the north would have been used by those coming from the harbour. Various courts separated the buildings, the most impressive being the Central Court. The private rooms were situated in the East Wing of the Palace called by Evans the Domestic Quarter, now more usually known as the Residential Quarter. To the north of the private rooms were workshops and storerooms mostly situated on a lower floor. The West Wing across the Central Court contained storage rooms, shrines and cult rooms, and most probably state apartments.

When Evans started to excavate, Kefala Hill was already well known as the site of a Bronze Age Palace. Minos Kalokairinos had made soundings in twelve different areas in the central part of the West Wing between December 1878 and February 1879 (pp. 37, 55). He kept some of the pottery in his house and this was studied, published in part by various scholars and widely discussed. A Turkish Bey had also dug in the south-east corner of the Palace, the West Magazines, and north of the Residential Quarter. In 1881 W.J. Stillman visited Knossos and reported to the Archaeological Institute of America on the ancient walls and huge blocks of hewn stone incised with signs.

What was totally unexpected was the size of the Palace revealed by Evans' excavations. In common with Schliemann and others who wanted to excavate earlier, Evans assumed that the whole Palace was contained in what was in fact only the West Wing. He started to dig in the south-east corner of this wing and worked north. It would have been a dramatic moment when he realised (as he soon did) that the Palace was much bigger than had been thought and extended east beyond the Central Court (called in the early days of the excavation the East Court). Over the succeeding seasons Evans continued to work south to north in the West Wing, west to east in the Northern Sector, then from north to south in the East Wing. The same scheme is generally followed here in describing the excavations (37ff).

There is little doubt that, in order to create an impression, Evans in many instances overstepped the mark and some restoration is mere conjecture. His work on the reconstruction of the Palace has always been a subject of controversy. In 1926 he read a paper to the Society of Antiquaries, which was published the following year in the *Antiquaries Journal* vol. vii, no. 3, 258–67. In this he explained and justified his methods, detailing the materials used and the problems encountered. This paper has been quoted at length throughout the booklet. As he pointed out 'To the casual visitor who first approaches the site and sees before him an acre or so of upper stories the attempt may well at times seem overbold, and the lover of picturesque ruins may receive a shock.

But the truth is that this supreme effort to preserve the record of the upper floors revealed by the process of excavation was from the first actually imposed on myself and my colleagues by the unique character of the remains with which we had to deal. The conditions were in fact quite different from those with which excavators have had to deal in the case of the mighty stone buildings of Egypt, or the massive brick structures of Mesopotamia, or of the somewhat parallel experiences to be met with on the Classical Greek and Roman sites'.

The Minoan collection is one of the 'treasures' of the Ashmolean Museum. Nowhere else outside Crete is it possible to study so much original material. The objects come from a variety of sources, but mainly through Sir Arthur Evans, some from his excavations, others collected by him over the years from 1894 when he first visited Crete. In his introductory notice to the Minoan section of the catalogue of the 1936 Jubilee Exhibition of the British School of Archaeology at Athens, Evans explained how he acquired objects from Crete. Before the Union with Greece in 1913 the Cretan Assembly gave him material, including a 'good representative series of the inscribed clay tablets from the Palace Archives' (pl. 28b). After the Union duplicate objects were ceded to the excavator. In addition, at the conclusion of the excavations, the Greek government presented a further series of objects which included fragments from the Taureador Fresco (pl. 41).

The story of Sir Arthur Evans' life and work is told by his half-sister Joan Evans in *Time and Chance, the Story of Arthur Evans and his Forebears* (1943) and by Sylvia Horwitz, *The Find of a Lifetime, Sir Arthur Evans and the Discovery of Knossos* (1981) and most recently by D.B. Harden in an Ashmolean publication, *Sir Arthur Evans: a Memoir* (1983).

The excavations were reported in the *Annual of the British School at Athens* vols. vi–xi (1900–1906).

A summary of the history of the site appears with extensive bibliography in M.S.F. Hood and W. Taylor *The Bronze Age Palace of Knossos; Plans and Sections*, British School at Athens Supplementary Volume 13 (1981).

Excavators and exploration funds

Sir Arthur Evans (Frontispiece *et passim*) began excavating at the Kefala hill, the Palace site at Knossos, Crete, on March 23rd 1900. From then onwards photographic records were kept as the work progressed: some were of specific features, others, more general, were taken from the specially built Observation Tower (pl. 3). Evans was fortunate in assembling a skilled team to help him in what was to become the main work for the rest of his life. He had little experience of excavating when he started to dig the site which he had purchased with so much difficulty (p. 22), but he was guided by D.G. Hogarth, then Director of the British School of Archaeology at Athens, who was to succeed him as Keeper of the Ashmolean Museum in Oxford (pl. 5a, 6a), and Duncan Mackenzie (see p. 18). Although Kefala was reserved for Evans to excavate, Hogarth worked on the prehistoric town and tombs at Knossos for two months before leaving to investigate the Dictaean Cave, one of the other sites in Crete earmarked for British excavations (pl. 6a). A year later Hogarth camped at Zakro in eastern Crete and excavated buildings there, but did not chance upon the Palace site which has recently yielded such spectacular results. A representative series of bronzes from the Dictaean Cave and objects from Zakro are now in the Ashmolean.

Theodore Fyfe, the architect of the British School at Athens, was to help Evans during the first five seasons at the Palace of Knossos, from 1900–1904 (pl. 6b). He was also able to visit the site intermittently over the following years. Fyfe became Director of the Cambridge School of Architecture (1922–1936) and University Lecturer in Architecture in 1926, a post which he held until his retirement in 1941; he died in 1945. In 1905, Christian Doll (pls. 7, 11) was employed as architect and was soon involved in the massive task of 'reconstituting' the Grand Staircase (77ff). In this he was helped by the practical advice of the Cypriot foreman, Gregorios Antoniou, who came to the excavation in 1902 (pls. 5c, 6a). 'Gregori' was a poacher turned gamekeeper; his youth had been spent tomb-robbing on Cyprus. He had been Hogarth's foreman for a dozen years working on British excavations in Cyprus and Crete, and later he was to go to the dig of the British School at Sparta.

Emmanouel Akoumianakis 'Manolaki' (pl. 8), took over from Gregorios

Exhibition arranged in Burlington House, London, 1936 to commemorate the fiftieth anniversary of the British School at Athens

1 Evans beside a cast of the throne from the Throne Room at Knossos (now in the Cast Gallery, Ashmolean Museum), and a jar decorated with an octopus (1911.608)

2 The North Room, 'Minoan', at Burlington House

3 Observation Tower built by the excavators at the south east edge of the Central Court

Antoniou as foreman. He was described in *The Times* (14.7.'51) as 'burly, genial, utterly devoted, [who] had descended on Knossos as a lad — "My mountain wolf" Evans called him — and made himself indispensable by an unusual flair for the antique, and by his administrative tact'. He was killed fighting during the invasion of Crete in the Second World War and is buried in the churchyard of the ruined little church of Hagia Paraskevi on the hillside overlooking the Palace. (The story of his death is pieced together by Dilys Powell, *The Villa Ariadne* (1973) 151ff.) Ever zealous in his protection of the site, Manolaki tried to prevent the graffitists defacing the Palace walls and was outraged when a party of French soldiers rode onto the site. Doll recorded in his diary on Monday March 12th, 1906, 'Row between Manolakis and the French Officer over their horses being taken onto the Excavation. Manolakis struck by the officer'.

Above all Evans was most fortunate in obtaining the services of Duncan Mackenzie (pls. 7, *et passim*), to whom he was to pay a generous tribute in the preface to vol. iv of the *Palace of Minos*. Mackenzie died in 1935, when the volume was still in the press, after a long and distressing mental illness which rendered him incapable of work. He came to Knossos with four years experience, 1896–1899, of excavating at Phylakopi on Melos, one of the Cycladic Islands. He had been summoned from Rome, where he was staying, by a telegram from Evans, 'Could you come superintend under my direction important excavation Knossos' ('believed Mycenaean Palace' was deleted perhaps to save words) 'Personal not school affair terms four months sixty pounds and all expenses paid to begin at once'. Mackenzie replied 'Agreed coming next boat'. A week later he started excavating at Knossos (p. 37).

On Melos, and later at Knossos, Mackenzie kept a day-book or diary of the excavations, extracts from which have been quoted below. Evans was to draw on them when writing up both the excavation reports and the *Palace of Minos*. Professor Renfrew, in his introduction to the Phylakopi notebooks, has pointed out that in spite of minor errors 'The Daybooks are nonetheless outstanding examples of systematic archaeological reasoning, produced at a time when scientific principles of excavation had not yet been established. Duncan Mackenzie was one of the very first scientific workers in the Aegean'. One of Mackenzie's talents was the ability to inspire the loyalty and interest of the workmen employed by Evans. Evans wrote, 'His Highland loyalty never failed, and the simple surroundings of his earlier years gave him an inner understanding of the native workmen and a fellow-feeling with them that was a real asset in the course of our spadework. To them, though a master, he was ever a true comrade'.

From the beginning, Evans insisted that the workforce on the site should consist of both Christians and Moslems. On an earlier visit to Crete he had visited Etèa, the scene of an appalling massacre by the Christians. Similar atrocities had been committed by the Turks against the Christians. He had witnessed the sufferings of both communities and had helped in taking aid to the destitute among them. The employment of men from the two sides, some lately involved in war, was Evans' very practical contribution to healing the breach. That the scheme worked was largely due to Mackenzie, who acted as master of ceremonies at the games and dances organised at Knossos on joint holidays (pls. 9, 10a).

Mackenzie was succeeded as Curator of Knossos by John Pendlebury during the season 1929–1930. During the next seven years Pendlebury worked at Knossos as well as directing the excavations at Tell el Amarna for the Egypt Exploration

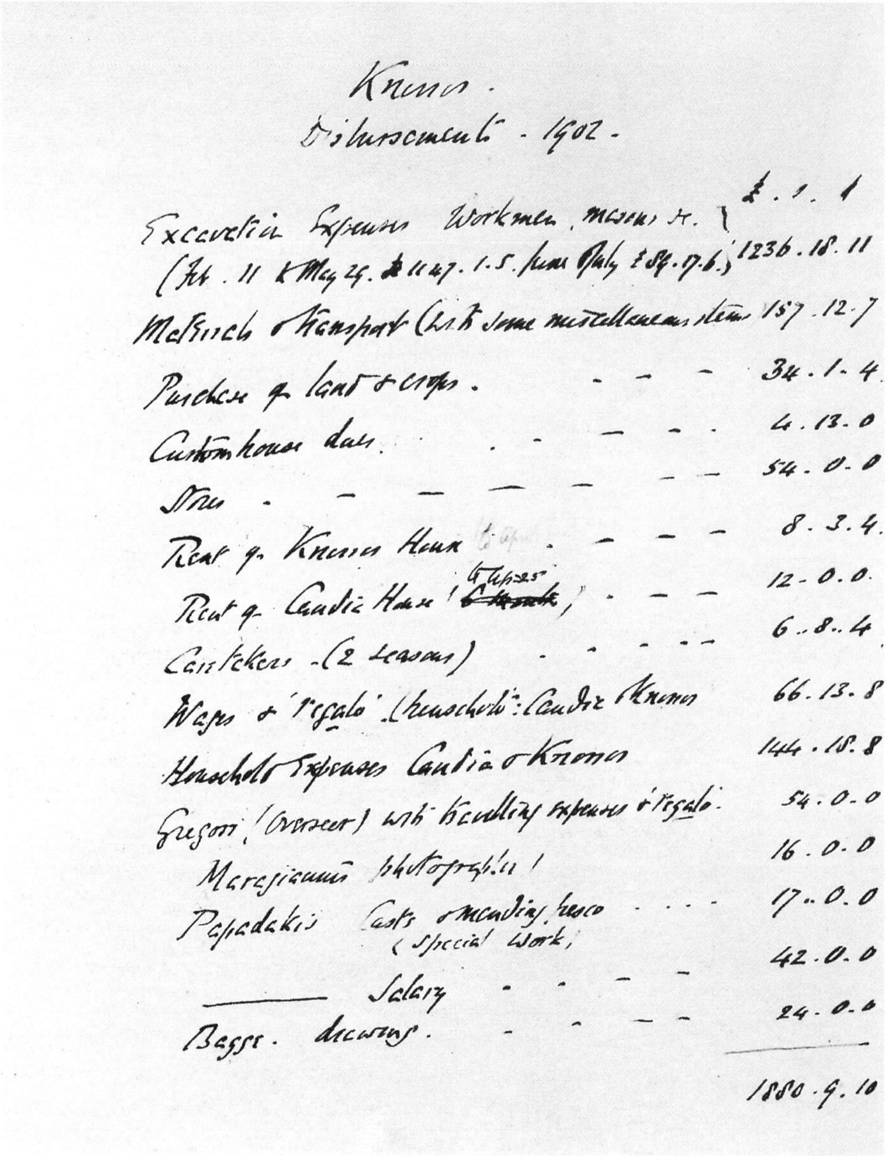

4 Knossos disbursements 1902. Entries include £71.17.8 for photographic work and a fee of £16 for Marayiannis; rental for the Knossos and Heraklion houses; payments to Gilliéron £76, Mackenzie with expenses £240, Fyfe £310 and Gregori £54.

Society. Evans had recognised his qualities and was glad of his support during his last years of excavation. Before he joined the army, Pendlebury was able to publish his important work in the Stratigraphical Museum at Knossos, a guide to the Palace and a more general book *The Archaeology of Crete* (1939). In 1940 Pendlebury was sent to Crete ostensibly to act as Vice-Consul. With the arrival of the British troops he was made Liaison Officer to work with the Greek forces. He was killed a year later during the airborne invasion.

Evans was also able to afford the services of a Swiss artist Emile Gilliéron (pl. 8) and later of his son, Edouard (pl. 11). Their artistic ability was stretched to the full in restoring and painting the reliefs and frescoes. Gilliéron *père* had already established an enviable reputation for himself when working for the French School at Athens.

A vast number of workmen and women were employed on the site including specialist carpenters and masons. Saturday was pay day and the workers usually stopped at midday. After 1906 they trooped up to the Villa Ariadne, which had been built as a convenient dig house by Christian Doll to Evans' specifications. The weekly ceremony can be seen in plate 10b. The men are gathered dressed in their baggy trousers, zouave jackets, headcloth or hat, belt and brightly coloured leather riding boots to receive their pay. In addition to their basic wage they were given extra for excellence and for finding objects, in theory to make them careful in case they missed some small find and thus the chance of a bonus. In 1900 the average wage for a day's work was eight piastres, or one shilling and four pence: the bonus ranged from one to eight piastres. At one time as many as three hundred men and women were employed, the women sieving the earth and washing and sorting the pottery (pl. 12a).

Wages and the building of the Villa Ariadne were not the only calls on Evans' resources (pl. 4). Finance was to occupy a major part of his thoughts throughout his work at Knossos. The fact that he was a rich man's son, and, after Sir John Evans' death and that of his cousin Tom Dickinson in 1908, an extremely wealthy man in his own right, profoundly influenced the work at Knossos. There is absolutely no doubt that without his personal wealth there would have been no question of excavating Knossos in the way it was done, and even less of restoring the Palace, because the expense of the latter particularly came largely from his own pocket. Indeed Evans bought the site of Kefala with his own money long before he inherited his fortune. The negotiations for the land were extremely complicated

5a Evans and Hogarth outside the rented house at Candia
5b Evans at Candia
5c Gregorios Antoniou on his mule

6a Hogarth (*right*) and Gregorios Antoniou (*far left*) outside the Dictaean Cave

6b Theodore Fyfe and workmen in the Hall of the Double Axes in 1901

and the political situation so unstable that it took several years to complete the purchase. Evans finally succeeded where others, including Schliemann, and Joubin of the French School, had lost interest or failed. In 1894 Evans acquired one quarter of the site: the final bill appears not to have been settled until 1896 (pl. 13). In 1895 he was back in Crete enjoying looking at his share and trying to purchase the other three quarters. In 1896 he, as owner of part, was trying to compel a sale and gave formal legal notice, signed with a Cretan seal, of his intention. The political situation worsened and in 1897 Evans visited Sardinia and North Africa instead of Crete. In 1898 Crete became independent under a High Commissioner, Prince George of Greece, appointed by the Great Powers, Britain, France and Russia. At last with a more favourable political situation it seemed as if the sale for the remaining three quarters of the land would go through. Dr Joseph Hazzidakis, President of the Society for the Promotion of Education, and at this time concerned with the archaeology of the Island, who had been holding a watching brief for

7 Evans, Doll and Mackenzie (*behind*) standing on the steps of the Villa Ariadne in 1910

Evans, wrote — in rather ungrammatical French — that the co-proprietors were willing to sell; 'Maintenant ils sont bien disposé à vous céder la terrain de Kefala à un prix raisonnable. D'après leur paroles j'ai compris que vous pouver achete les trois quarts avec une somme de 200£ .. Et comme vous appartienne la quatrième partie vous serais le maître de toute la Kefala'.

In 1894 Evans had specified that money for the purchase of Kefala would be forthcoming from the Cretan Exploration Fund, which was at that time non-existent. In June 1899 it was announced that a Cretan Exploration Fund was to be established under the aegis of the British School of Archaeology at Athens to raise money for the excavations of Evans, Hogarth and other British archaeologists on Crete. George MacMillan, a life-long friend of the Evans family, was its treasurer. In 1900 Evans and Hogarth jointly signed a letter appealing for funds, which appeared in the newspapers, but, as they well knew, the times were not propitious. An appeal brochure was issued at the same time (pl. 14). 'The preoccupation of the public mind caused by the war in South Africa made it impossible last year to press the claims of Cretan exploration. Sympathy, indeed, was not wanting. A representative Committee was formed, and we were able to initiate a Fund, to which the patronage of the High Commissioner of the Powers in Crete, Prince George of Greece, was accorded. Thanks to the good offices of his Royal Highness, a number of important sites were set apart for British excavation. But of the £5,000 required for the adequate realisation of our scheme, barely a tenth part was collected by private subscriptions.

The sum of about £500 which had been privately collected, was devoted to the furtherance of two separate enterprises. Half of the amount went to assist Mr Arthur Evans in the excavation of a site, already acquired by him at Kefala on the site of Knossos, which proved to contain the remains of a prehistoric Palace. How inadequate was this contribution may be judged from the fact that five-sixths of the cost of the work — still far from completion — have fallen on the explorer's shoulders'. A glance at the list of subscribers shows that the Evans family had already donated about £150 of the £513 collected. The other half of the money went to Hogarth for the excavations of the prehistoric town and tombs of Knossos and of the Dictaean Cave. The British School at Athens had contributed £200, 'spared with difficulty'. Now a further £3,000 was needed to continue the excavations. 'The clouds of war are at last lifting, and it is with confidence that we now appeal for help to carry on the work already in hand'. A small grant was made by the British

8 Gilliéron *père* standing on the steps of the Villa Ariadne; Manolaki sits on the balustrade wearing a wide brimmed hat

Association amongst other bodies, and appeals for public subscriptions, organised by George MacMillan, continued over the years. But the public was slow to respond and a large part of the monies needed came either out of Evans' own pocket, or, in the early years, from handsome donations from his father Sir John Evans, who responded generously to his son's telegrams telling of some spectacular find by sending money.

Finance was the cause of friction between Evans and Hogarth. Hogarth was not a rich man and naturally had to draw a salary and expenses, of which Evans had no need. Evans, curiously insensitive to his feelings, rather despised Hogarth for this

27

9a Preparing for the tug of war. To right Mackenzie in dark suit, Fyfe, and Evans facing camera.

9b A tug of war in the Central Court

10a A dance

10b Pay day at the Villa; at the right of the picture Evans and Mackenzie sit at the foot of the steps, Gregori, now bearded, looks on

and an acrimonious correspondence ensued. Hogarth wrote 'These expensive methods are yours in digging, as in collecting and in ordinary life. You are a rich man's son, and have probably never been at a loss for money' (Joan Evans, *Time and Chance*, 341). He also pointed out that Evans' expensive life style and the 'princely' way in which things were done did not encourage subscribers to contribute, especially when they had the frugal example of Flinders Petrie before them. Work was done *per alios* which others had to do *per se*. *Per alios* included not only Mackenzie but also an architect (paid for by the British School), considered essential on a dig today but when Fyfe and Doll were at Knossos somewhat of a novelty. F.G. Newton, the architect who worked at Ur, was later to draw for Sir Arthur, and in 1922 Piet de Jong was appointed and continued to be involved with the site, serving as Curator of Knossos from 1947 to 1952, until his death in 1967.

The first house that Evans rented for the excavating team was at Knossos. It belonged to the Turkish Bey or landowner of the area. The situation, near the south-east corner of the Palace site, proved unhealthy and after the first season the excavators were based on a house in Candia (Heraklion) until the Villa Ariadne was built. Something is known of the social life of the team from the diary of 1906–7, left by Christian Doll when he was working continuously not only on the Villa Ariadne, but also on plans of the Palace (worried that his measurements did not always agree with Fyfe's) and daily administration. A British garrison was stationed at Candia and various regiments were posted to Crete. Evans certainly dined in the Officers' Mess and no doubt strolled down to the square to listen to the regimental bands on a Sunday. Doll tells of countless dinner parties, and it evidently became fashionable for the soldiers and officers and their wives to drive or walk out to Knossos and visit the excavations. Sometimes the soldiers were not merely content to look (pl. 43b). A considerable part of Doll's time was taken up with visitors. On one occasion he entertained the Camp Choir to tea in the Hall of the Colonnades. The Throne Room was used for smaller groups and other visitors were entertained at the house at Candia. In addition to these more social occasions, there were visits from other archaeologists. Good Friday, April 13th 1906, must have been a daunting day for Doll: 'Came out to Knossos early and saw that the Excavations were being cleaned up properly. Only Moslems at work. Finished off the ruined wall better next the door bases on Upper East West Corridor. Profs. Mosso and Pernier on the Excavation quite early. Prof. Gardner and party arrived at 1 o'clock in 4 carriages. Showed him all the unsafe spots to be avoided. Showed

Wace over the Palace Staircase. Gave the party tea at the Candia house'.

Luigi Pernier was one of the Italian excavating team working at the Palace of Phaestos near the south coast of Crete. Professor Mosso, an anthropologist, also worked at Phaestos. Professor Ernest Gardner, one time Director of the British School at Athens (1887–1895), was one of the scholars who organised cultural tours through Hellenic waters and visited various archaeological sites. He had brought a party to Knossos during the first season's work. Alan Wace, who was born in 1879, had joined the British School in 1902. He was to become Director 1914–23, later being appointed as Laurence Professor of Classical Archaeology at Cambridge. Wace and Evans were to become protagonists in a lengthy controversy over the question of possible Cretan domination of the mainland and in particular of Mycenae where Wace, following in Schliemann's footsteps, excavated at Evans' instigation.

There were also visits by members of the Archaeological Congresses, to whom Evans wished to lecture and offer entertainment, and individual archaeologists such as Professor Dörpfeld, Schliemann's chosen collaborator and successor at Troy, Director of the German Archaeological Institute at Athens. With such scholars he was able to discuss the excavations. The visitor whom Evans must have most enjoyed entertaining was his father who, in 1901 at the age of seventy-seven, had come to Knossos to see for himself the work to which he had been subscribing.

Evans was an autocrat and, as we have seen (p. 27), somewhat insensitive to the feelings of those working with him, yet he inspired loyalty and affection. His enthusiasm and humour were infectious. Christian Doll who had suffered much from his peremptory letters and orders wrote to the Keeper of the Department of Antiquities, Dr Harden, on December 8th 1951 on the occasion of the Evans Centenary Exhibition held in the Ashmolean Museum, 'I am the last survivor of the original team that worked with Sir Arthur at Knossos and I still have lively recollections of those times. There certainly never was a more delightful man to work or live with. His energy and his sense of humour were a constant source of admiration to me. I count it a great privilege to have known him so intimately'.

Evans' enthusiasm extended beyond the finds and excavations. His lively notebooks are very different from the rather dull diary of Christian Doll. He was deeply influenced by natural surroundings and his love of flowers led him to create the wild flower gardens round Jarn Mound, near Oxford. He describes the flowers and scenery of Crete in several passages in his travel diaries. On Friday March 30th

11 Gilliéron *fils* sitting on the balustrade, Doll standing on the bottom step and Mackenzie in the doorway of the Villa Ariadne, 1910

12a Women washing sherds in the Central Court outside the Anteroom of the Throne Room

12b Evans and Mackenzie watching workmen at the south dump; in the background the Acropolis hill, Monastiriako Kefali

1894 he visited Kamares, the cave, where polychrome pottery which came to be known as Kamares Ware was first found. It is dramatically situated high on the southern slope of Mt. Ida, visible from Phaestos. Evans' diary entry reads 'The rain at last stopped. Off to Kamares over and along an offshoot of Ida. Wind tremendous. Several times almost blown off the horse, and the horse repeatedly blown off the track! ... From Kamares descended by an exquisite gorge with oleander thickets growing along the side of a roaring stream — magnificent olives of hoar antiquity starting up among the rocks — and such an array of anemones from white to scarlet and every shade of blue and purple — pink and rose madder — below the heights of Ida — before us the glimpses of the Messara plain and the Libyan Sea'. The people he met and their houses were amusingly described and he was not above entering the menu of a meal he had enjoyed at Pyrgos where the Chief of Gendarmerie entertained him to dinner:

Soupe au riz (with lemon) *Pilaf with yaourt*
Kebabs à l'huile   *Melon*
Irish stew à la Turque   *Eau de la Source*

13 Receipt for the quarter share of Kefala which Evans bought

His excavation notebooks are full of drawings of the objects that interested him, but they are somewhat scrappy and difficult to use. Half filled pages are sometimes used up for drawings of objects from other areas or found at different dates. But they are important for identifying objects and their provenance. Many of the objects in the Ashmolean were identified from the notebooks by Professor Boardman when he was Assistant Keeper in the Department of Antiquities (1956–1959). There are revealing glimpses also of how Evans changed his mind as further excavation brought fresh evidence to light, or when he had discussed his ideas with visiting scholars, or with the 'experts' he called in. Quite frequently an entry reads 'long conference with Mackenzie'.

Even in his serious writings Evans had a colourful turn of phrase and a romantic outlook. He gave the Palace rooms and areas imaginative names which, far easier to remember and identify than numbers, immediately conjure up a picture of their possible uses. His lectures likewise were imaginative. At Wootton (see p. 12) in 1906 his talk about the Knossos excavations was entitled the 'Magic of the Spade' and the notes for opening read — 'The magic of the spade has called up a forgotten world. The old tales have come true — Minos — Ariadne — Theseus — The Tribute Children — the Minotaur itself'. His vision of the Palace as the home of the legendary King Minos led him, with a sense of fun, to call the 'lustral basin' in the Throne Room 'Ariadne's bath' in his notebook and the throne 'Ariadne's throne' (p. 40). The Throne Room was also known as the Council Chamber of Minos. The theme was taken up in a leading article in *The Times* (5.11.1900) — 'Archaeology is the Ariadne which has at last furnished the clue' to what lies at the root of Hellenic Civilization.

The Palace for Evans was not just an archaeological site but an imposing residence inhabited by people very alive to him. In the *Palace of Minos* vol. III, 301 he wrote — 'During an attack of fever, having found, for the sake of better air, a temporary lodging in the room below the inspection tower that has been erected on the neighbouring edge of the Central Court, and tempted in the warm moonlight to look down the staircase-well, the whole place seemed to awake awhile to life and movement. Such was the force of the illusion that the Priest-King with his plumed lily crown, great ladies, tightly girdly, flounced and corseted, long-stoled priests, and, after them, a retinue of elegant but sinewy youths — as if the Cup-bearer and his fellows had stepped down from the walls — passed and repassed on the flights below'.

Evans in his Wootton lecture described the excavations at Knossos — 'Suppose one stood in the middle of a field and said "I have an open sesame" the ground will open, a Palace will appear'. Indeed the excavations did appear to be touched by magic but the results were only accomplished by a lot of hard work coupled with Evans' flair. Mackenzie was to begin his excavation day-book for 1900 more prosaically (p. 37).

The Cretan Exploration Fund.

Patron:

H.R.H. PRINCE GEORGE OF GREECE,

High Commissioner of the Powers in Crete.

Directors:

ARTHUR J. EVANS, M.A., F.S.A.,
Ashmole's Keeper, and Hon. Fellow of Brasenose College, Oxford.

DAVID G. HOGARTH, M.A., F.S.A., F.R.G.S.,
Fellow of Magdalen College, Oxford, and late Director of the British School at Athens.

R. CARR BOSANQUET, M.A., F.S.A.,
Director of the British School at Athens.

Hon. Treasurer:

GEORGE A. MACMILLAN,
Hon. Secretary of the Society for Promoting Hellenic Studies.

Hon. Secretary:

JOHN L. MYRES, M.A., F.S.A., F.R.G.S.,
Student of Christ Church, Oxford.

The Throne Room in the Palace at Knossos in course of Excavation.

The following Appeal, including a Statement of last Season's work, has been issued on behalf of the Fund:—

THE preoccupation of the public mind caused by the war in South Africa made it impossible last year to press the claims of Cretan exploration. Sympathy, indeed, was not wanting. A representative Committee was formed, and we were able to initiate a Fund, to which the patronage of the High Commissioner of the Powers in Crete, Prince George of Greece, was accorded. Thanks to the good offices of His Royal Highness, a number of important sites were set apart for British excavation. But of the £5,000

14 Title-page of the appeal brochure issued by the Cretan Exploration Fund in 1900; excavating the floor of the Throne Room

The Excavations

Duncan Mackenzie's day-book entry for Friday 23rd March 1900 reads — 'The excavations by Mr Arthur Evans at Knossos began this morning at 11 a.m.'. When Mackenzie arrived after lunch there were 32 men and a foreman at work. By April 1st a hundred men were employed. The first season's excavations were to uncover about two acres of the Palace site. But before the work could begin a dumping ground for the earth removed had to be found. The site chosen was to the south and east (pl. 15). Some of the dumps were found to cover part of the Palace and later had to be moved (pl. 16). One of the season's most dramatic discoveries was that of the Throne Room and the excavation and restoration of this can be seen in pls. 17–27.

The Throne Room

The ground in this area had evidently been little disturbed since the final destruction of the Palace, as only a few inches below the surface parts of walls with frescoes still adhering to them began to appear (pls. 18–19, 22). The Throne Room complex was excavated in the usual manner by the gradual removal of successive layers of earth carried away in baskets to wheelbarrows and then dumped. It was found that the complex consisted of an Anteroom, Throne Room and a small back chamber or Inner Sanctuary or Shrine. The Anteroom or Lobby (Minos Kalokairinos had cleared part of this area in 1878–79) was entered from the Central Court by a short flight of steps: a narrower stepped entrance gave access from the north. Traces of original plaster still covered the steps and part of the Anteroom floor when excavated. Benches ran along the north and south walls: above the south wall bench a fresco fragment was later identified as showing a bull's hoof: other fresco fragments showed panels imitating veined stone. Between the benches along the north wall charred remains of some wooden object were found, perhaps a throne as Evans has restored it.

The west end of the Anteroom gave access to the Throne Room. A large stone-lined tank (Evans jotted down 'Ariadne's bath') or lustral basin, the bottom of which was reached by six steps, ran along the south wall (pl. 17a). A number of in-

15 Knossos looking west from Ailias in 1901. The Throne Room is already roofed, and sherd dumps are in the foreground

16 Knossos looking west from Ailias in 1902. The dumps have been moved, the Lobby of the Wooden Posts partially restored, a landing block of the Grand Staircase raised and the retaining wall of the Central Court built

lays of crystal and other materials was found in the basin, which Evans thought had probably fallen from a Loggia above (a Loggia was restored in 1930). The north side of the Lustral Basin was bounded by a parapet above a bench, in which were sockets for columns. The charred traces of the wooden columns still remained. On the floor near the north east corner of the Throne Room was a large plain 'pithos', or jar, overturned and lying on its side (pls. 18, 22a): round it were a number of low-shaped 'marble vessels' (pl. 17b). A similar vase was found in the opposite corner, the position marked in Evans' 1900 notebook (pl. 17b). Two of these alabastra, heavily restored, and a fragmentary lid, are now in the Ashmolean (pls. 20a, 21). There is some uncertainty about the number of stone alabastra found in the Throne Room. Professor Warren has traced at least eight definite pieces and fragments of up to four more which may come from the Throne Room. Evans in 1913 noted the marks where vases had stood on the floor of the passage behind the 'bath', and also of alabastra by the throne: but he only drew and mentioned four, plus a 'cover', in his stone vase notebook, noting that a similar alabastron had been found in a passage by the Stone Vase Room. The alabastra usually had spiral decoration round the rim and figure-of-eight handles. More inlay fragments were found near the Throne, some of which seem to have come from a stone-lined cavity in the north wall (pl. 22a). Fragments were also found inside this 'loculus' or niche when it was cleared. A selection of inlays found in the basin and on the floor and now in the Museum collection is illustrated (pl. 21).

On the north wall, only about 0.30 m from the surface, was part of a fresco which Evans recorded on April 13th as showing palms (next day he was to add 'No! reeds'). Next to the fresco Mackenzie states that there 'appeared a tall slab in the wall and this on further clearing proved to be the back of a stone chair whose seat was soon brought into view' (pl. 22b). The chair, throne, or seat of honour, was set on a small platform and originally had been covered with painted plaster. One of the witnesses to its excavation was Harriet Boyd, the American pioneer archaeologist who, encouraged and helped by Evans and Hogarth, was travelling round Crete looking for a site of her own to excavate. She visited Knossos and notes in her diary that Mr Evans dubbed the chair 'the Throne of Ariadne' (*Archaeology* 18, pt. 2 (1965) 97). The throne had a wide moulded seat which Evans considered was more suitable for the ample proportions of a woman, than a man. It was of elaborate design with curving lines and crockets which he thought looked 'almost Gothic'.

wooden copies made by an Oxford joiner for his house Youlbury, on Boars Hill, near Oxford. Two now stand in the Ashmolean's Arthur Evans Room. It is said that he gave others as wedding presents to his young friends.

The west wall had an entrance from the Throne Room to the small Inner Sanctuary. A considerable area of fresco still adhered to this wall, although part had slipped down onto the bench and floor below (pls. 18–9). Parts of seated griffins — they were identified as such by Gilliéron *père* when he visited the Throne Room on April 18th — could be seen flanking the entrance. Evans noted the use of hatched lines to represent shading on the griffins' bellies. When he duly reported this to the press, *The Times* misunderstood and noted that a griffin hatching eggs was depicted. On the 13th February 1902 a griffin's paw was identified to the right of the Throne on the north wall. Evans had previously interpreted this as part of an eel. As late as 1973 Sinclair Hood and Joseph Shaw identified a large piece of fresco as coming from the dado of the west or north wall. There has been a good deal of speculation about the restoration of the griffins in the Throne Room. Mark Cameron has recently pointed out that there is evidence for three griffins and that while significant details of the restoration are certainly wrong the general scheme with its four griffins is likely to be correct (pl. 22c).

In June, at the end of the first season's excavation, it was clear that some sort of cover would have to be erected over the Throne Room if the gypsum floor, benches and the plaster fresco fragments which had not been removed were to be preserved. The solubility of gypsum varies. The gypsum selected by the Minoan builders for the Palace floor was exceedingly tough and has resisted the wear of feet and water remarkably well. It is not clear where this durable gypsum was obtained. Gypsum available locally at the hill of Gypsades was highly soluble in water and easily destroyed. As gypsum was more colourful than the limestone also used in the Palace construction it was frequently utilised to decorate many of the interior parts of the Palace, although surprisingly it was sometimes covered with plaster. In addition to its decorative qualities, it could be cut easily, perhaps with the large bronze saws then in use. A small bronze saw in the Ashmolean is illustrated (pl. 20b).

The Throne Room was to be re-roofed three times. A roof was completed as a matter of urgency early in 1901. A flat roof was built (pl. 24), and in order to support this, columns were fitted into the positions formerly occupied by the Minoan columns, whose burnt remains were found *in situ*. The restored columns were covered with plaster and painted, the work being supervised by Theodore Fyfe (pl. 23a,b,). In order to prevent unwelcome visitors entering the newly roofed Throne Room, wrought iron railings and iron gates made by a blacksmith in Candia were erected (pl. 24). In 1904 the flat roof was replaced by a more permanent pitched construction using metal girders for support (pl. 25). The loft was fitted up with shelving and baskets for sherds as 'a kind of reference Museum'. The Throne Room was finally restored in 1930 when the entirely modern upper storey was constructed using reinforced concrete (pls. 26b, 27). The upper floor was used as a 'picture gallery' for replicas of the frescoes from various parts of the Palace (pl. 22d). Three facsimiles of griffins were added to an earlier griffin (restored in 1913) by Gilliéron *fils*, in the Throne Room itself (pl. 22c).

To the south of the Throne Room a Stepped Portico led up from the Central Court. The illustrations show how this was built up over the years until in 1923 the 'complete restoration including a supporting column, of the first flight of the Grand Staircase on the West, above the Stepped Portico of the Central Court' was recorded by Evans in *The Times* August 8th (pls. 25–27). The steps led to the upper floor or Piano Nobile and a further flight gave access either to a second floor or the roof. Mackenzie thought, probably wrongly, that two slabs forming a 'seat' in the Room of the Chariot Tablets (pl. 28a) were steps from here.

17a The lustral basin in the Throne Room in 1900. The remains of a charred wooden column at the top of the steps.

17b The Throne Room, Evans Notebook, April 14th, 1900. The steps at the bottom right in Evans' drawing correspond to the steps on the left hand side of the photograph.

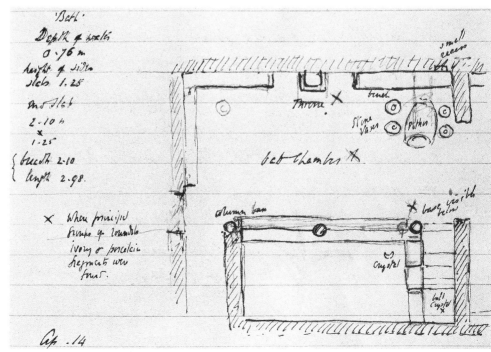

18   The Throne Room looking west in 1900. An overturned jar lies on the floor, and fresco still adheres to the wall to the right of the throne and on the west wall where part has slipped onto the bench and floor

19   The Throne Room looking west from the Anteroom after the floor has been cleaned. The stone basin in the foreground came from a passage to the north. Evans stands beside a tent

20a Two gypsum alabastra decorated with spirals round the rim, from the Throne Room (1911.611; AE.767), both restored (*c* one sixth actual size)

20b A bronze saw with three rivet holes for attaching a handle (1910.179) (*c* one sixth actual size)

21 Lid of a gypsum alabastron (AE.768), and objects of faience (1910.179), crystal (1938.547-560; 1941.71) and stone (1938.467) from the Throne Room (*c* one half actual size)

22a The Throne Room in 1900 showing a niche in the north wall and fresco to the right of the throne and on the east wall

22b The throne; the dado above has been restored and the fresco fragments removed to Heraklion Museum

47

22c The Throne Room as restored in 1930

22d The gallery above the Throne Room used for displaying replicas of frescoes from various parts of the Palace

23 Restoring the Throne Room in 1901. Wooden columns were fitted into the original Minoan sockets, covered with plaster and painted; brick pillars and a flat roof completed the structure.

24 The Throne Room in 1901 showing the flat roof and wrought iron
gates. To the west is the Long Corridor giving access to the West
Magazines; to the south parts of the stairs of the Stepped Portico leading up
from the Central Court, and the Temple Repositories next to the Room of
the Tall Pithos (a medallion pithos remains in place). To the west behind
these two rooms lies the Vat Room. The Room of the Chariot Tablets is in
the foreground to the far left of the photograph

25 Looking west from the Central Court when a pitched roof had been constructed on the Throne Room (1904) and the Stepped Portico partially restored at a later date

26a The Throne Room, Anteroom and Stepped Portico taken from the Central Court looking west in 1900

26b The Throne Room complex restored in 1930 and to the south leading up from the Central Court the Stepped Portico restored in 1923

52

The Temple Repositories

Further to the south again, next to the Room of the Tall Pithos, lay a small room excavated in 1900. In the floor were two open cists, or vats, evidently used for storage, with the upper borders cut out so that lids could be fitted and secured (pl. 30a). 'At that time' [1900] wrote Mackenzie in his day-book for May 28th 1903 'nothing of much interest was found', but in 1903 it was noticed that the floor in the room was sinking and it was decided to lift the paving and investigate. Two deep repositories or stone lined cists, the Temple Repositories, were found with Middle Minoan pottery and 'treasures'. From the surface down to a depth of between 1.10–1.20 m a large quantity of vases was found closely packed together, 'the two prevailing types being the amphora and the pitcher' (pls. 29, 30b). When the sherds and complete vessels were washed and sorted it could be seen that some were decorated with birds in a style 'not Knossian'. Mackenzie was able to identify them without hesitation as native Melian, as he had found similar ware during the excavations at Phylakopi on Melos. After about 1.20 m the deposit changed and a variety of small objects came to light in both repositories, particularly the larger eastern cist. These included sealings or seal impressions, ivory and bone objects, shells both real and in faience, beads and inlays, a selection of which is now on display in the Ashmolean (pl. 30c). Among the more spectacular finds were a marble cross and faience figures of a snake goddess and votaries. Part of one of these statuettes was found in the east repository and a joining fragment came from the western cist which also held quantities of gold leaf. The whole deposit was removed for sieving so that no object however small could be missed. It was possible to leave one of the later cists in position for it lay directly above a partition between the two repositories.

The Vat Room

Behind the Temple Repositories lay the Vat Room (Room of the Stone Vats) entered from the East Pillar Room, which had evidently been used as a store room because vats, rectangular chests, were sunk into the floor, and there were the remains of several pithoi. In 1903 a small pit under the pavement of the entrance to the room was investigated and a number of vases and vase fragments was discovered (pl. 31).

The Room of the Chariot Tablets

Evans had been drawn to Crete in the hope of tracing a prehistoric system of writing. The clues that led him to the island accumulated over the years. In 1893 when visiting antique shops in Pandrosou, Athens, he had seen seal stones with hieroglyphic inscriptions and was told that they came from Central Crete. In Candia he was shown an impression of a four-sided hieroglyphic seal again from Central Crete. The original seal was in the Ashmolean Museum presented by Greville Chester and incorrectly labelled 'from Sparta'. In 1895 he saw a clay tablet of a type he was to call Linear B. It was owned by a chemist, Kyrios Zachyrakis, and may have come from Minos Kalokairinos' excavations, but unfortunately it was lost in the 1898 rising against the Turks.

In the very first days of the excavation, on March 30th 1900, part of 'a kind of elongated clay bar, rather like a stone or bronze chisel in shape though broken at one end, with script on it and what appear to be numerals' was found. A few days later a small 'archive' room, south of the Temple Repositories and adjoining area, which came to be known as the Room of the Chariot Tablets was investigated (pl. 28a). A hoard of tablets came to light. Remains of carved wood, sealings and seven bronze hinges were excavated with the tablets, suggesting that the hoard had been stored in wooden chests secured with string and sealed. One of the tablets from this hoard is illustrated (pl. 28b). Since the decipherment by Michael Ventris (see below) the tablet can be read — Meunas, a personal name or title of an official, precedes the ideograms for a corslet (long recognised as such but dramatically confirmed now by the discovery of a bronze corslet at Dendra on the Greek mainland) and for a chariot. The tablet probably records the issue of equipment to a charioteer. Linear B inscriptions, so-called by Evans, occur on clay tablets, labels and sealings and occasionally painted on vases. It was not the only system of writing found at Knossos. A pictographic script seems to have flourished at the beginning of the Middle Minoan Period and at some point within the same period Linear A was developed. The advanced type of Linear B script was used in the Late Minoan Period to keep the Palace records and establish ownership. The Palace was an important administrative and economic centre with an elaborate system of bookkeeping. Evans tried in vain to decipher the script. It was not until a decade after his death that Michael Ventris, who had been inspired by his Jubilee lecture in 1936 (p. 11), identified Greek forms in the Linear B texts.

The West Magazines

To the west a Corridor 53 metres long can be seen running north–south. This Long Corridor gave access to a series of 18 narrow storerooms or Magazines which bordered the west side of the Palace. In many of the storerooms huge clay storage jars or pithoi were found (pls. 32, 33b,c, 34a). It has been estimated that the average sized jar held about 35 gallons. Olive oil, wine, grain or pulses could be stored equally well in such vessels. Asquith, in a speech at the annual meeting of subscribers to the British School at Athens (reported in the press, October 29th 1900), describes this 'long succession of magazines containing gigantic store jars that might have hidden the Forty Thieves'. Evans in 1900 was not the first to investigate the area, as Minos Kalokairinos in 1878–9 had found twelve pithoi in the Third Magazine (pl. 33a), some of which he had distributed. One was given to Crown Prince Constantine of Greece, and is now in the National Museum, Athens. Others are in the British Museum, the Louvre and in Rome. Those that he kept were destroyed with the rest of his collection when his house was burnt to the ground in the rising of 1898. His brave son Andrea also perished in the fighting. Kalokairinos had pointed out the areas of his excavation to Evans when they visited the site on March 21st 1894.

The huge medallion pithos now in the Ashmolean came from the Tenth Magazine which had been disturbed by treasure hunters (pls. 32, 34a). This was probably 'one of the two rare pithoi in the 10th Mag' which Mackenzie wrote and told Evans (7.6.'05) 'was overturned by some careless visitor and smashed'. In 1910 Heaton, Doll and Mackenzie rode out to see itinerant potters at work on the slopes of Mt Juktas (pls. 34b, 35a). They watched modern pithoi being made, several at a time; a wheel was turned by hand by the potter's assistant seated in a hole in the ground, and the pithoi were gradually built up from the clay base (pl. 34b). Doubtless much the same method of manufacture was used in the Minoan period. Pithoi were extremely versatile and could be used for a variety of purposes other than storage. In the Middle Minoan period a pithos was often used as a burial urn. A pithos in a photograph taken in 1910 (pl. 35b) is in use as a chimney-pot, and others were used as dog kennels or hen coops.

Below the later floor of the Second Magazine Evans found a vase damaged by the later builders; inside it were several smaller objects, including a small spouted jug (pl. 36). Some of the small cups had fine earth and charcoal still inside them. Extra wide walls between some of the Magazines suggest that these supported an upper storey, and column bases were also found. Evans restored a floor in reinforced concrete and the columns of a Great Hall over some of the Magazines. This seems to agree with the evidence. The restoration of two other rooms is perhaps not so certain.

The Khyan Lid Deposit

A later blocking wall had been built across the Long Corridor, beyond which lay Magazines XIV–XVIII. At the end of the Long Corridor, beyond the Terrace wall, lay a complex area and here a few metres to the west of the North Lustral Basin the excavators found an alabaster lid. The lid was inscribed with a cartouche containing the name of the Hyksos pharaoh, King Khyan in Egyptian hieroglyphs. The lid seemed to be of great importance in establishing a *terminus post quem* for the Late Minoan Period, but lately the date of the deposit in which it was found has been questioned and the danger of using imported stone vases for dating emphasised. The exact find place, in spite of the apparently careful notes by Evans in his notebook and the diagram in the *Palace of Minos*, is still not entirely clear. A considerable number of stone vase fragments came from the same deposit. Two restored vases are now in Oxford (pl. 37). One is a limestone ewer with relief plaitwork probably imitating leather thongs or basketry; the other is a bridge-spouted bowl with round white inlays. Similar fragments were found in the North Lustral Basin a few metres away.

The North Entrance Passage

To the north east lay one of the main entrances to the Palace. This North Entrance was a complex structure, basically a paved passageway through high bastions, which was altered at different phases of the Palace building. The photographs (pl. 38) tell their own story. The Charging Bull fresco fragments were found in 1900 and a replica was erected on the West Portico in 1930. The spouted jar with light on dark decoration (pl. 38 d) comes from the so-called Guard Room near by.

Evans posed for a photograph taken by a neighbour from Oxford, Raymond ffennell of Wytham Abbey, in the North Entrance in 1922 (pl. 39). He had joined the ffennells on their yacht *Halcyon* at Nauplia and after a gruelling sea-trip, Evans, who was an extremely bad sailor, took the party to Knossos where he talked about the excavations. Hazel ffennell, then aged seventeen, who had already endured Alan Wace, Director of the British School at Athens, lecturing at various sites on the

27a The Stepped Portico with stairs and columns restored in 1923

Greek mainland, including a two hour discourse on the Acropolis at Athens, was not particularly impressed. Perhaps she would have preferred to have seen Knossos after 1930 when the restoration was complete. She wrote in her diary, quoted in *Hazel* (edited H. Allan) 92, 'Knossos, not quite a heap of stones as usual but on the verge thereof, lies on the slopes of a hill overlooking the slopes of another, and a winding road. There are many stone staircases leading into different chambers, none of which latter can really be called palatial, and a great many earthenware vases for holding treasure, and a small throne of King Minos, were about the best things there!'

27b   View from the Central Court looking north west over the Stepped Portico, the Throne Room complex and the Charging Bull fresco restored on the West Portico of the North Entrance Passage in 1930

28a Room of the Chariot Tablets in 1900

28b A Linear B tablet from the Room of the Chariot Tablets (1938.704)
(*c* 1½ times actual size)

29 The Temple Repositories investigated in 1903. One of the later cists lies between the two deep repositories. Pitchers and amphoras are ranged round the room

30a The two later cists above the Temple Repositories

30b Vases, including imported Melian bird jugs, from the Temple Repositories (AE.807-08; AE 852, 855, 1507, 1828-29, 1938.866) (*c* one tenth actual size)

30c Part of a breccia hammer (1936.589), clay sealings (1938.1439-40), and a faience shell, inlay, arm with a bracelet round the wrist (AE.1201.1 1938.541-2, 697), and beads (1938.529 1941.214) from the Temple Repositories (*c* one half actual size)

31 Vases from the Vat Room Deposit including Cycladic ware (AE.1070; 1072-76; 1078; 1097-8; 1177 and 1941.189) (*c* one quarter actual size)

32 West Magazines IX and X in 1901

33a Evans and Mackenzie looking across the Long Corridor
to the entrances of the first West Magazines

33b West Magazine IX

33c West Magazine IX

34a A large Medallion pithos from West Magazine X, (AE.1126)
(*c* one tenth actual size)

34b Itinerant potters at work on the slopes of Mt. Juktas in 1910

35a Doll and Mackenzie visiting a pottery on the slopes of
Mt. Juktas in 1910

35b A pithos used as a chimney-pot on a village house at
Megalouvrysis in 1910

36a A large damaged jar, from beneath the floor in Magazine II (AE.974). Inside were a number of smaller vessels including a spouted jug (AE.977) (*c* one sixth actual size)

36b Page from Evans' 1900 Notebook showing drawings of some of the objects found beneath the floor of Magazine II including the spouted jug (AE.977)

36c Early photograph of AE.974 and AE.977 and several other small cups, nodules of clay and flakes of obsidian, also found in AE.974

In the third gallery W. just below to Myc-
floor level was a large pot with Kamáres
decoration in white but containing small vessels
of apparently later date. Some were small cups
with pea nuts or charcoal in them & a small
another // painted ear & cup. There
were also several curious nodules of market clay

Clay nodules

buff & reddish
brown stripes

Object inside Kamáres pot.

Stone vases from the Khyan Lid Deposit

37a-b A grey stone ewer with ring collar and plait-work relief decoration, restored with one handle; originally there may have been two (AE.850) (*c* one quarter actual size)

37c A brown stone hole-mouth jar with round white inlays (AE.835) (*c* one fifth actual size)

38a   Excavating the North Entrance Passage in 1901

38b   The North Entrance Passage in 1901

38c The West Portico of the North Entrance Passage, restored with the Charging Bull fresco in 1930

38d A spouted jar with light on dark decoration, from the North Guard Room (AE.846) (*c* one ninth actual size)

39 Sir Arthur Evans standing in the North Entrance Passage in 1922, photographed by Col. Raymond ffennell

The Royal Pottery Stores

Few traces of the Later Palace remained in the eroded North East area and a Roman pottery kiln had disturbed the ground. Nearby a whole series of store rooms belonging to the Early Palace was investigated. The rooms were used for storing pottery of such high quality that they came to be known as the Royal Pottery Stores (North East Kamares Area) (pl. 40). The bowls and cups found were of the thinnest egg-shell fabric and because they were so fragile most were broken. Fortunately many could be restored. Some had painted decoration, others were impressed with patterns; both shape and patterns seem to derive from metal vessels and the slight metallic lustre found on the black impressed ware recalls the appearance of silver (pl. 40).

The Taureador Fresco

The Taureador Fresco comes from the East Wing of the Palace. The fragments illustrated here (pl. 41), restored by E.J. Lambert, were given to Evans by the Greek Government. The Court of the Stone Spout (Court of the Oil Spout) was excavated in 1901 (pl. 42a). It was probably originally an open space. Later two walls were built running east–west and butting onto a fine limestone wall, which stood five courses high when excavated. In the fourth course there was a 'square projecting gargoyle', or stone spout which gave the court its name. The fresco fragments were found in the upper layers of *débris* in the south west corner. Further fragments emerged when the later rubble walls were cleared in 1902. Perhaps the fresco once decorated a room above the adjoining Schoolroom. The fragments belong to several panels within decorative frames. Each panel evidently depicted a scene from the bull-games, which were held perhaps in the Central Court or below the East Wing of the Palace. It was possible to restore one panel with some confidence. This shows a girl grappling with a bull: a boy somersaults over its back and a second girl stands behind ready to help. The exciting discovery was to find that girls took part in the bull-games. The common convention of using white paint for female flesh and red for male distinguishes the girls from the boys. The girls have their hair dressed in curls over their foreheads and are also more gaudily dressed. Both sexes have long tresses and are dressed in belts or loincloths, striped 'socks', pointed shoes and wear bangles and necklaces. Their hands are bound with thongs like boxers. The cowgirl in the Ashmolean is shown in back view twisted round (pl. 41a).

Noel Heaton joined Evans during his 1910 campaign to study the frescoes. He found that not only the interior walls were plastered, but also floors, stairs and at any rate some external and light well walls. Even some of the 'beautiful gypsum slabs' were covered. He visited other sites in search of evidence, notably Hagia Triadha and Phaestos and took several samples. It appears that a fine lime plaster was applied to rubble walls over a backing of coarse mortar of rubble lime and clay with about fifty per cent broken sherds and chips of stone. The walls which were constructed of limestone blocks or gypsum were plastered direct without the coarse layer. The lime was obtained by burning limestone. Heaton visited the labyrinthine quarries at Hagia Irini near Knossos, accompanied by Evans and Mackenzie, and the photograph (pl. 42b) was probably taken there. These quarries however, were almost certainly not exploited during the Bronze Age.

Heaton found that the colours used were, as he expected, simple earth pigments. The walls of the Earlier Palaces had been covered with red painted plaster, sometimes with simple designs depicted in red or white. In the Later Palaces painted scenes were frequent and far wider ranges of colours were used. White was obtained from lime; the black was a carbonaceous shale or slate; red and yellow were iron oxides. The blue pigment came from two different sources. One was the Egyptian Blue and manufactured; the other was natural and has recently been identified as glaucophane by using modern X-ray analytical techniques. Glaucophane-bearing metamorphic rocks exist on Crete, but not near Knossos. Heaton wrote in *The Architect and Contract Reporter* (14.4.'11) 'The paintings lined the walls and floors of the stately rooms and corridors of this magnificent palace, which must have been daily thronged by multitudes of people from all parts of the then known world'. He considered that the paint must have been applied in true fresco technique while the plaster was still wet. The main outlines were inscribed on a wet plaster as a guide, and the outlines of the figures were then sketched in. The background was given a uniform wash, usually of yellow or blue, and finally the details of the figures were added. Only enough wall was prepared as could be covered while the plaster was still wet. The plaster was kept ready, probably in broad-mouthed storage jars. Such jars were found at Thera with the plaster still *in situ* and nearby were two pebble rubbers for grinding the pigments. The pigments dried out with the plaster, hardened and became firmly bonded.

Most of the frescoes were removed from the walls and taken to the museum at Heraklion, being replaced eventually on the Palace walls by replicas. Evans described the process of removal and cleaning with dilute hydrochloric acid in his 1900 notebook. They were removed by undercutting, accompanied by the gradual introduction of plaster to the back and edges. The plaster set and the fresco could then be lifted. This use of plaster, however, has made the work of restoration and conservation difficult.

The Loomweight Basement

South of the Court of the Stone Spout lay small rooms, one of which was named the Loomweight Basement. From this room came a 'pithos-amphora' decorated with white palms on a black background (pl. 43b). Half of this vase is in Heraklion Museum, the other half in the Ashmolean. Evans explains in the *Palace of Minos* I, 253 note 3, how 'The fragments of one side were taken to England by a British Officer (at a time when the local Cretan administration withheld even duplicate specimens from the excavators)'. A miniature cup, amphora and one-handled jug (pl. 43a), as well as many loomweights, came from the same area.

The Town Mosaic

At a higher level in a small narrow room fragments of faience plaques were found in 1902. Perhaps they once decorated a wooden chest. Most of the inlays were broken and badly rubbed, but some have been restored (pl. 44). The plaques represent houses of different types and towers and other buildings — a 'Town Mosaic' — which gives evidence of the homes of ordinary Minoan citizens. There appear 'to be two doors, divided by a central panel, an arrangement superficially suggestive of modern semi-detached villas. Above the doors are two double windows filled with bright red pigment, above that again two larger window openings, and finally, what looks like an attic, with a small single window also coloured red' (*Annual of the British School at Athens* vol. viii (1902) 16). The dots evidently represent the ends of wooden beams.

The Lobby of the Wooden Posts

A little to the south, still on the east slope, lay the Room (Lobby) of the Wooden Posts. The photographs (pls. 45–46) plot the excavation and restoration. As reconstructed the original woodwork is in coloured concrete. The centre post supports the huge stone block which was found *in situ* in 1901 held up by *débris*, which included the charred remains of a wooden post.

The Corridor of the Bays, The Grand Staircase and
The Hall of the Colonnades

In May 1901 the workmen were excavating in a wide passageway running north–south in the Residential (Domestic) Quarter, which came to be known as the Corridor of the Bays. Massive masonry piers divided the corridor into bays or recesses which had been used for storage (pls. 47–48). By the evening of Saturday May 11th three recesses had been completely cleared. Duncan Mackenzie thought that a fourth and fifth recess lay beyond, and he recorded in his day-book 'recess 4 is not yet completely excavated, the interior of the recess is encumbered by large fallen blocks making excavation extremely difficult'. Over the next few days steps began to appear and it became clear that a 'dramatic development of the excavation — discovery of the Grand Staircase' was slowly unfolding. Bay 4 was found to be a landing at the meeting point of the East West Corridor and the Corridor of the Bays, from which stairs ascended and descended. On May 16th Mackenzie noted 'the considerable depth of the floor level in Bay 5 lends great importance to the whole adjoining neighbourhood, this being the greatest depth at which a floor-level has as yet been found on the site'. The floor of 'Bay 5' was reached at c. 4.50 m and proved to be the landing between the first and second flights of steps of the Grand Staircase. By May 22nd the stairway leading south from the landing ('Bay 4') to this landing ('Bay 5') was found to have twelve steps (pls. 49, 55a). On the east side there was a dangerously bulging wall (see below) (pl. 49).

From the first landing ('Bay 5') further steps led down east. These were thought to lead directly into a large chamber, the Hall of the Colonnades, which was also being excavated (pl. 51b). Two days later an attempt was made to tunnel through from the steps into the Hall, but it was abandoned as being too dangerous. In fact there was no entrance at this point and it soon became apparent that more steps led down north to a lower level giving access to the Hall of the Colonnades. This first flight of stairs presented a great problem, as it underlay, in part, the third flight which, flanked by a balustrade with sockets for columns, still remained *in situ* (pls. 49–51). The only way to dig out the first flight was to tunnel. Evans wrote in the *Annual of the British School at Athens* vi (1900–1901), 'It was altogether miners' work necessitating a constant succession of wooden arches'. Luckily two of the workmen on the site had been miners working the ancient silver mines at Laurion south east of Athens and they were able to advise on the tunnelling and method of shoring up the walls and roofs with wooden props. After eight days a passageway was cleared down the steps and air vents cut through the rubble wall into the adjoining Hall of the Colonnades. This rubble was not removed until 1905 but formed the support for the upper flights of stairs and balustrades. Originally the west end of the Hall was unroofed providing a light well for the successive stories; a drain carried off the surface water. A window in the south wall lit a small private staircase. The window had collapsed and was filled with fallen masonry but the wall still stood eleven courses high (pl. 51).

The reasons for the remarkable state of preservation of the Grand Staircase and the Hall of the Colonnades are described by Evans in the *Antiquaries Journal* vii (1927) 258f — 'At Knossos from the earliest stage of the excavations it became evident that, over and above the ashlar and rubble masonry of the walls, we had to deal with a solid wooden framework, in which much of it was cradled, and with wooden posts and columns supporting the massive beams above. This wooden skeleton had been reduced for the most part to mere charcoal, in a minor degree, however, by actual conflagration and clearly to a much larger extent by a chemical process of carbonization.

It might perhaps be concluded from this that, the supporting and binding power of this original framework having been removed, the whole building would have collapsed into a confused heap. It is evident that in almost all cases the upper floors have sunk, in a certain measure owing to the decay of the lateral supports inter-calated in the surrounding walls. But the remarkable and recurring phenomenon that presented itself was that, in spite of all this, throughout a good deal of the West Quarter of the Palace and to a still greater degree in the "Domestic Quarter" on the East slope, as well as in many of the surrounding private houses, gypsum paving slabs, door-jambs, limestone bases, the steps of stairs, and other remains came to light on the upper level, almost at the height at which they had originally rested, though the intervening supports, such as the wooden posts and columns that had originally raised them above the lower floors, were reduced to brittle masses of charcoal.

In the "Domestic Quarter" the maintenance of upper storey remains, more or less at their original level, was no doubt helped by the fact that it was built into a great cutting in the hill-side and had received a good deal of lateral support. But this itself was far from explaining the at first miraculous evidence of upper storey remains that we there encountered, which has made it possible to recover an almost perfect plan of the first floor.

The problem is seen under its most striking aspect in the "Hall of the Colonnades", where the balustrade on the North side was found as it were suspended almost at its original level, while the triple balustrade of the upper flight of stairs on the West side is seen to rest on a mass of clay and rubble, the supporting columns having been in both cases carbonized and disintegrated.'

This clay and rubble mixed with dissolved gypsum produced a hard concrete-like substance, which provided a support.

The 1901 season's excavation was drawing to a close. A vast area had already been uncovered and a start had been made on restoration and preservation. But a foretaste of future disasters occurred on the night of June 11th when the wooden props supporting part of the balustrade of the East West Corridor overlooking the Hall of the Colonnades and part of the tunnelling proved unequal to the strain (pl. 50).

The following year, 1902, the problem of the dangerously bulging wall had to be tackled (pl. 49). 'A very serious problem was presented by the upper dividing wall of the Grand Staircase of this Quarter; it had heeled over and threatened ruin, not only to itself, but to the outer staircase and the rising balustrade above it. Professional guidance ceased at this point but, as the case seemed desperate, I took upon myself the responsibility of what might be thought a very risky operation. A slit was first cut along the base of the mid-wall on either side, the whole wall was cased with planks and roped round, a block of timbering was constructed to stop the movement of the wall at the point where it became perpendicular, and, these preparations having been made, a body of sixty work-men on the terrace above, under the skilled direction of Gregori, was harnessed by ropes to the casing of planks round the masonry and at a given signal pulled as one man. It was a moment of breathless excitement, but the great mass moved all together, righted itself, and stopped on the line fixed for it. The slit on the inner side of the wall was thus closed. That on the outer side was filled in at once with rubble and cement, and the work was done,' (*Antiquaries Journal* vol vii (1927), 261–62).

Another labour-consuming task had then to be faced. The stone blocks which formed part of the Grand Staircase had in many cases 'been thrown into the void, and one of the most arduous tasks encountered in the way of reconstruction was the raising of these to the positions that they had originally occupied ... This could only be done by an arrangement of inclines, with very solid planks, up which the blocks were levered, pushed, and pulled with the aid of ropes by gangs of work-men' (pl. 52b). The huge block which would have been above the middle landing was found to have the marks of the top of the steps of a fourth flight of stairs and 'at the cost of much labour this important block has now been replaced in the position that it had occupied previous to its fall' (*Annual of the British School at Athens* vol. viii (1902), 33) (pls. 53, 55a).

In 1905 disaster struck again. Mackenzie wrote 'On our return this season found heavy winter rains which had done much damage in the villages in different parts of Crete had also left their mark in different parts of the Palace of Knossos'. On April 6th he again wrote 'It was at once apparent that unless strenuous measures were taken at once the whole upper fabric of the stair might collapse'.

The work was made even more urgent because members of the Archaeological Congress in Athens were expected to visit the site, as MacMillan stressed in *The Times* (12.4.'05) — 'Mr Evans is naturally anxious to be able to show so distinguished a company of scholars all that can still be seen of the famous Palace. Accordingly Mr Doll, now acting as architect to the British School at Athens, has been sent for specially to attend to this work. But this reconstruction involves serious and unforeseen expenditure, and so far will diminish the already scanty funds available for further researches'.

The course of the restoration and the discoveries which occurred during the work were set out by Evans in an article in *The Times* (31.10.'05). 'An exceptionally rainy season led to the falling in of the second landing of the Grand Staircase. The wooden props inserted at the time of the excavation to support the upper structure of this — which, in default of the original wooden pillars, simply rested on indurated *débris* — had given way at this point and the whole of the upper flights and balustrades together with the adjoining upper corridor, were threatened with ruin. To avert this demanded nothing less than heroic measures. The tunnel below the third flight of stairs, by means of which a narrow gangway had been obtained up to the underlying first flight, being rendered insecure, it was necessary to remove provisionally the steps and balustrades above belonging to the third flight — to be subsequently replaced at their original level when properly re-supported. The upper structures once removed, the remaining *débris* that had underlain them could now be cleared away, an operation which resulted in a most illuminating discovery. Below the stepped balustrade that accompanied the upper flight of stairs, and separated from it by an interval of fallen and carbonised materials, there came to light on the outer border of the lower flight another similar ascending balustrade with sockets for columns like those above and even the charred remains of the actual wooden shafts.'

The wooden props were replaced by stone columns fitted into the orginal sockets; these were plastered over and painted (pls. 54a, 55b). They were modelled both for shape and colour on the columns depicted in the fresco fragments from a hall in the West wing of the Palace discovered in 1904. Iron girders, set in cement, imported at great expense and with some considerable difficulty (particularly in the unloading at Candia harbour when many fell into the sea), were used in place of the original architraves and beams. Much later a new mole was constructed by Robert McAlpine & Sons which offered safer harbourage. To quote again from *The Times*, 'The actual size of the architraves and beams could be ascertained from some large charred sections actually preserved .... The basis of this reconstruction must in any case be held to be secure .... The stones moreover of the upper flights of stairs and of their balustrades had been carefully marked and numbered so they could be re-set in their original positions. It was found necessary to carry out the same reconstruction under the adjoining Upper Corridor and across the Hall of the Colonnades which the Grand Staircase overlooks — the partially collapsed masonry above the window in the south side of the Hall being at the same time raised, the window itself opened out, and its original wooden frame replaced' (pl. 55b). Evans reporting on the sixth campaign at Knossos wrote in *The Times* (31.10.'05): 'The result achieved by this legitimate process of reconstitution is such that it must appeal to the historic sense of the most unimaginative. To a height of over 25ft there rise before us the Grand Staircase and columnar hall of approach practically unchanged since they were traversed 3½ millenniums back by kings and queens of Mino's stock on their way to the more private quarters of the Royal household. We have here all the materials for the reconstruction of a brilliant picture of that remote epoch. The colonnades standing out against the glittering gypsum dados and the painted frieze above (of which portions have now come to light) with its linked spirals and rosettes; the ascending flights of stairs — to which fresh evidence supplied by two corner blocks now enables us to add a fifth; the low convenient balustrades that accompany the stairs, tier above tier, upon which, as in the miniature frescoes from the North Hall of the Palace, we seem to see the Court ladies in their brilliant modern costume with pinched waists and puffed sleeves seated in groups and exchanging glances with elegant youths in the court below —

dark-eyed these, with dark, flowing locks, sinewy, bronzed, and bare of limb save for the tightly-drawn metal belt and ornaments, and their richly embroidered loin-clothes. A note of mystery is added by the window, now freed from *débris*, in the wall to the right, which opens on to the landing of another and more private stair-case. Here surely — if fancy indeed may transport her to a sublunary scene — at times may have looked out that Princess of most ancient romance whose name is indissolubly linked with the memories of Minoan Knossos'.

In 1910 further work on the Grand Staircase was undertaken. Investigations included raising some of the paving at the foot of the stairs (pl. 54b), but the major work was in restoration. Duncan Mackenzie, now the Director of the Palestine Exploration Fund, was again Evans' assistant. Doll was able to superintend some serious structural work and Gregori was foreman. Evans reported in *The Times* (16.9.'10) '... An interesting development took place which greatly extended the architectural scope of these undertakings. Before the discovery of the Grand Stair-case, remains of a series of somewhat angular gypsum slabs had been found on the eastern border of the Central Court, and their importance at that time not being recognized these had been laid along the edge of an exploratory shaft and sub-sequently lost sight of under the wooden cover that had been placed over it as a precaution. But this cover now to be replaced and the gypsum slabs being thus once more brought to light, their meaning at once became apparent. They were, in fact, the remains of the steps of the fourth flight of the adjacent staircase. The massive landing blocks of this were in their places, showing marks on their sides left by some of the missing steps, and the re-discovery of the gypsum slabs has made it possible to replace the greater part of five steps of this fourth flight in their original position. This unexpected result encouraged us to undertake the more arduous task of setting up in their places the great landing blocks of the fifth flight of stairs, which had come to light at a lower level during the original excavation. This involved the cutting out and socketing of two additional stone columns to support the blocks (pl. 56a,b); but Mr Doll was equal to the occasion, and the blocks both of the upper and lower landing of the fifth flight of the Grand Staircase have been successfully placed in their original position' (pls. 56a,b).

In 1928 the Loggia of the Grand Staircase was restored and roofed over. A replica of the Shield Fresco, the painted shields representing spotted cattle hides stretched over frames, was executed by E. Gilliéron *fils* (pl. 56c). The reconstruction which extended to the Hall of the Double Axes was supervised by Piet de Jong.

The Hall of the Double Axes

There was no direct access from the Hall of the Colonnades to the Hall of the Double Axes which lay immediately behind it to the east. The entry to this area was from the Lower East West Corridor. The west wall of what was apparently the Hall's light well stood eight courses high and was built of large blocks, rising up to 4.50 m or a little over 13 ft (pl. 57), on which were incised many of the double axe signs which gave the greatest of the Palace Halls its name. The Hall of the Double Axes was excavated in 1901. Two column bases were found 65 cm in diameter and the remains of two cypress columns, one of which was 2.60 metres long. To the east of the light well were two rooms and a portico or verandah across the east and south east sides. Oblong bases with double reveals and half bases against the north and south walls showed the position of the dividing pillars, walls and doors. Immediately above the western bases corresponding bases, supported by *débris*, were found 3.50 metres higher. The course of their excavation can be seen (pl. 58). When the *débris* was hacked away the upper bases were temporarily removed and then supported by wooden scaffolding (pl. 59a). The following year, 1902, wood and stucco pillars were made to replace the scaffolding. These rested on the original bases. In 1908 Christian Doll had to replace much of the decaying wood with iron girders and stonework. At the same time the window between the light well and the Lower East West Corridor was cleared of about six tons of fallen masonry and the lintel was restored. It was not until 1928 that major reconstruction took place. Before that date it had been considered far too expensive to think of roofing over the Hall. With the introduction of reinforced concrete, however, this became feasible. Piet de Jong supervised the work which was spread over five months. The whole of the Hall of the Double Axes including the porticoes was roofed over, and the upper floor was relaid at its original height. The following year zinc shields were made to hang between the replica spiral fresco on the south wall.

The Queen's Megaron

A dog-leg corridor led from the Hall of the Double Axes (the King's Megaron) to the smaller Queen's Megaron (pl. 59b) which was to be restored with the Dolphin and Dancing Girl frescoes. Beyond the Queen's Megaron lies the south east area of the Palace which had suffered a considerable amount of damage at the end of the Middle Minoan period and was much eroded at the time of its excavation. The photographs of this area are therefore fewer and less informative.

This picture book makes no attempt at a comprehensive description of the photographs in the Ashmolean which include many from areas not described here, and Homer's 'broad Knossos' consisted of much more than the Palace. Evans investigated many of the surrounding houses, the harbour area, roads and cemeteries and many of these excavations are recorded in the notebooks and photographs.

By 1930 Evans' controversial reconstitutions were completed. He returned to Crete the following year, crossing from Piraeus by sea-plane, and with John Pendlebury and Piet de Jong excavated the Temple Tomb. In 1935 he was again in Crete (pl. 60) and was honoured at Knossos, when in distinguished company and with elaborate ceremony a bronze bust was unveiled; the following day he was made an honorary citizen of Candia and crowned with a laurel wreath. This was to be his last visit to the island and six years later he died at Youlbury, his house on Boars Hill, Oxford.

40 Cups restored from fragments found in the 'North East Kamares Area' which came to be known as the Royal Pottery Stores of the Old Palace. A polychrome cup of egg-shell ware imitating stone (AE.947); a bowl of similar fabric with 'racquet and ball' decoration in red and white (1929.405); a bowl 'of extraordinary thin fabric, embossed arcading derived from the fluting of bowls in precious metals: the arcading is surmounted by small fleur-de-lis' (1938.561); sherds with impressed decoration (AE.935;937) (*c* one half actual size)

41a A girl taking part in the bull sports on restored fragments from the Taureador fresco (AE.1708) (*c* one quarter actual size)

41b Fresco fragments showing a male taureador (AE.1707) (*c* one quarter actual size)

42a The Court of the Stone Spout in 1901 showing later walls built abutting the west wall on either side of the spout; fragments of the Taureador fresco were found in the upper *débris* of this area. Blocks of the Grand Staircase are in the background

42b A visit to the quarry of Hagia Irini in 1910. From left to right, Kosta, Evans, table server, Doll, Mackenzie behind local guides, and Manolaki

43a　Three miniature vases from the Loomweight Basement (AE.1241; 1938.585-6) (slightly reduced)

43b　A large jar decorated with a triple group of palm-trees, from the Loomweight Basement (AE.1654), restored; the other half of the vase is in Heraklion Museum (*c* one eighth actual size)

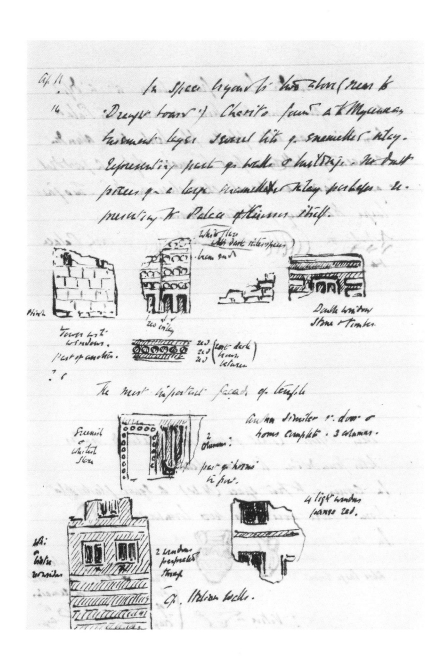

44a A page from Evans' Notebook, April 11th 1902, with drawings of the Town Mosaic

44b A faience inlay from the Town Mosaic (actual size, 1936.591)

45a Excavating the Lobby of the Wooden Posts, 1901. The stone block is shored up with wood props. The block in the background is from the Grand Staircase

45b Workmen standing against the *débris* which supported the stone block in the Lobby of the Wooden Posts in 1901

45c Looking west in 1901. On the right is the Lobby of the Wooden Posts, and above a landing block of the Grand Staircase. Part of the stairs leading to the upper East West Corridor lies to the left, and to the far left the Hall of the Double Axes.

46a The Lobby of the Wooden Posts partially restored.

46b Upper East West Corridor looking west

46c The Lobby of the Wooden Posts after
restoration in 1930; to the left the entrance to the
Portico of the Hall of the Double Axes

47 Vessels from the Corridor of the Bays
(AE.817-19,1180) (*c* one quarter actual size)

48 A page from Evans' 1901 Notebook with
drawings of vases from the Corridor of the Bays

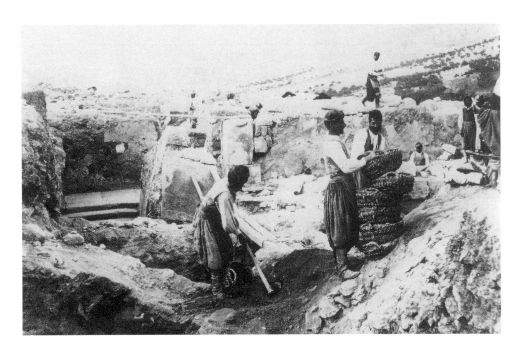

49a Excavating the area of the Grand Staircase in 1901, the bulging wall and steps of the second flight on the left, a plank lies across the entrance to the Corridor of the Bays, part of the balustrade of the third flight, to right the Hall of the Colonnades

49b The same view of the Grand Staircase, facing north, taken later in 1901

50 To the left the balustrade of the third flight of the Grar Staircase above the rubble-filled west wall of the light well the Hall of the Colonnades. The balustrade of the East Wes Corridor overlooking the light well is propped up on wood scaffolding, 1901

51a Looking west, the balustrade of the third flight of the Grand Staircase with sockets for columns *in situ*. A restored pillar with the landing block of the fourth flight erected in 1902; the bulging wall was straightened in the same year. Below to the left the south wall of the Hall of the Colonnades with blocked window, and drain

51b Excavating the Hall of the Colonnades in 1901 with the blocked window in the south wall, and rubble-filled west wall of the light well

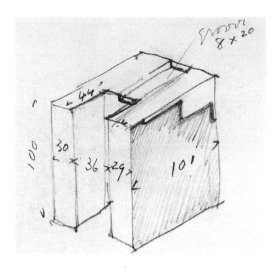

52a A drawing of the landing block with a groove and marks of steps on the side; by Theodore Fyfe in 1902

52b Doll supervising the re-positioning of the landing block of the fourth flight of the Grand Staircase perhaps in 1905; the block was first raised in 1902

53 Restoring the Grand Staircase probably in 1905. The wooden props are being replaced by iron girders, and the rubble from the west wall of the light well of the Hall of the Colonnades has been removed and columns fitted into the original sockets. Evans in a white pith helmet stands on the third flight of stairs; next to him is Mackenzie and in front Doll wearing a wide-brimmed hat

54a The first flight of the restored Grand Staircase with the columns plastered and painted. Rubble, removed in 1905 revealing the lower balustrade, once filled the area where the child sits

54b Evans and Doll watching workmen lifting the pavement at the foot of the Grand Staircase. On the wall to the right high above Doll's head a piece of fresco remains *in situ*

55a View from above the Central Court looking down on the Grand Staircase. Wooden props still support the East West Corridor and the lower flights of stairs. The photograph was taken between 1902 and 1905

55b Looking west over the light well of the Hall of the Colonnades, with the window in the south wall cleared and restored

56a   The Grand Staircase looking south after 1910 when the great landing blocks of the fifth flight were restored with two additional columns to support them

56b   The Grand Staircase after restoration in 1910

56c   In 1928 the Loggia overlooking the light well of the Hall of the Colonnades was restored and a fresco incorporating shields and spirals executed by Gilliéron *fils*

57 The Hall of the Double Axes looking west in 1901. The west wall still stood a little over 13ft high

58a Evans, wearing a pith helmet, watching the excavation of the Hall of the Double Axes in 1901

58b A chain of workers removing baskets of debris from the Hall of the Double Axes in 1901

58c Bases of the upper floor of the Hall of the Double Axes being excavated in 1901

59a Looking east over the Hall of the Double Axes in 1901; the bases have been replaced and propped up by wooden scaffolding, and high upon the north wall fragments of fresco have been carefully protected by wooden casing

59b The Queen's Megaron looking west

60 Evans on his last visit to Knossos in 1935

Select Bibliography

The Palace at Knossos

Alexiou, S. *A guide to the Minoan Palaces: Knossos — Phaestos — Mallia* (Heraklion, n.d.)

Cadogan, G. *The Palaces of Minoan Crete* (London, 1976)

Evans, A.J. *The Palace of Minos at Knossos* I-IV with Index volume (London, 1921–36. Reprinted 1964)

Graham, J.W. *Palaces of Minoan Crete* (Princeton, 1962)

Hallager, E. *The Mycenaean Palace at Knossos* (Medelhavsmuseet, Memoir 1, Stockholm, 1977)

Hood, S and Taylor W. *The Bronze Age Palace at Knossos* (Supplementary Volume 13 published by the British School at Athens, 1981)

Mosso, A. *The Palaces of Crete and their Builders* (London, 1907)

Palmer, L.R. *The Penultimate Palace of Knossos* (Rome, 1969)

Pendlebury, J.D.S. *A Handbook to the Palace of Minos at Knossos* (new ed., London, 1934)

Raison, J. *Le Grand Palais de Knossos. Répertoire photographique et bibliographie* (Rome, 1969)

Shaw, J.W. *Minoan Architecture: materials and techniques* (*Annuario della Scuola Archeologica di Atene* 49 (1971), Rome, 1973)

The excavations were reported in the *Annual of the British School at Athens,* particularly vols. vi–xi (1900–1906), also in the *Journal of Hellenic Studies, Antiquaries Journal* and *The Times.*

General

Higgins, R. *Minoan and Mycenaean Art* (London, 1967)

Hood, M.S.F. *The Minoans, Crete in the Bronze Age* (London, 1971)

Hutchinson, R.W. *Prehistoric Crete* (Harmondsworth, 1962)

Pendlebury, J.D.S. *The Archaeology of Crete* (London, 1939. Reprinted New York 1963).

Sir Arthur Evans

Evans, J. *Time and Chance: the story of Arthur Evans and his Forebears* (London, 1943)

Harden, D.B. *Sir Arthur Evans: a Memoir* (Oxford, 1983)

Horwitz, S. *The Find of a Lifetime, Sir Arthur Evans and the Discovery of Knossos* (London, 1981)